Color Your W a Life You Love™

HEAL YOUR
BURNED-OUT
SELF

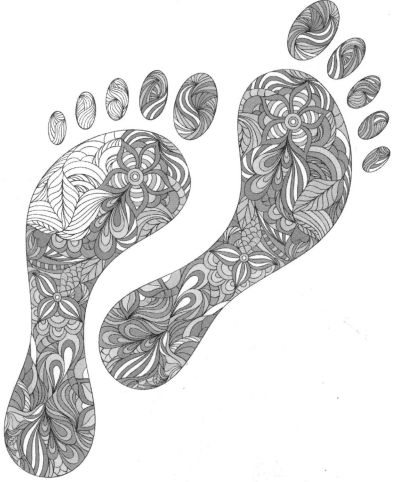

A SELF-HELP ADULT COLORING BOOK
FOR RELAXATION & PERSONAL GROWTH!

60 CALMING DESIGNS TO COLOR!
FLOWERS & NATURE
ANIMALS
MANDALAS
DOODLES & PATTERNS

COLOR YOUR WAY TO A LIFE YOU LOVE™: HEAL YOUR BURNED-OUT SELF

For information:
shellijohnson.com
alphadollmedia.com

First Paperback Print Edition, December 2017

Published by Alpha Doll Media, LLC (the "Publisher").

ISBN: 978-0-9747109-6-9

WELCOME TO THE
COLOR YOUR WAY TO A LIFE YOU LOVE™
COLORING BOOK SERIES!

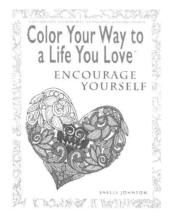

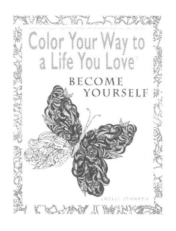

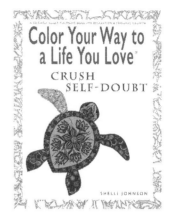

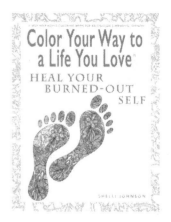

AVAILABLE NOW OR COMING SOON!

UNLEASH YOUR INNER CREATOR & MAKE IT YOUR OWN!

This is not just another coloring book, it's also an invitation for you to delve deeper into who you are so you can find out what makes you come alive. I'm a big believer in the power of taking small steps to get you anywhere you need or want to go. With that in mind, I invite you inside these pages on a creative self-help adventure. You'll unleash your artistic side with designs and patterns while you do daily small-sized activities aimed at: 1. helping you heal yourself and 2. inspiring you to create a life you love. My hope is that you'll use these pages to ignite your imagination, discard your limitations, and free your inner creator.

Feel free to add your own personal embellishments to any image. You can make each page as unique as you like by adding doodles, patterns, and/or shapes. Color the images any way you like with any tools you like. There are no rules except that you relax, enjoy, and color in a way that feels right to you.

THE MEANING & PURPOSE OF LIFE!

"The meaning of life is to find your gift. The purpose of life is to give it away."
—Pablo Picasso

THE PSYCHOLOGY
OF COLOR!

From my layman's understanding of the meaning of colors, certain colors can evoke certain emotions.

BLUE: centered, calm, hopeful, confidence
GREEN: growth, safety, endurance, calm
ORANGE: energy, happiness, encouragement, excitement
RED: passion, energy, strength, power, determination
YELLOW: joy, energy, cheerfulness
BROWN: stability
PURPLE: power, ambition, creativity, energy
BLACK: power, elegance, mystery
WHITE: light, goodness, safety

So keep that in mind as you color. If you're looking to experience a particular emotion/feeling/mood, you may want to use a particular color to help you get there.

A FEW HELPFUL SUGGESTIONS!

BABY STEPS
I'm a big believer in the power of taking baby steps to get you anywhere you need or want to go, which is why this coloring book is written the way it is. Each day has small-sized activities. They build on each other, one to the next. So feel free to color whichever image you'd like, just know you'll be best served to do the daily activities in order.

NO PERFECTION NEEDED
Do yourself a kindness and make a mistake in this coloring book early on. Scribble on some of the pages. Spill your favorite beverage on the cover. Rip one of the corners off. Color outside the lines. Make this book imperfect so that you'll feel free to be your real, honest self inside the pages. Being real, not being perfect, is what's going to heal you and set you free.

BE HONEST
I'd recommend that you don't show your answers inside this coloring book to anyone. Keep them to yourself for right now until you make it all the way through Day 30. Why? Honesty with yourself is what's going to help you heal and grow. You won't be completely honest if you're worried about someone reading your answers. In fact, what you're likely to do is tweak your responses, edit them, or scratch them out entirely if you're worried about how others might perceive you. So be kind to yourself & let this coloring book be just for you.

BE WILLING & OPEN
The first step to change is to be open & willing to it. You picked up this coloring book because you're struggling in this area of your life. If you want things to be different, well, both you & those things are going to have to change. So be open to experiencing something new & be willing to do the effort to get there.

GIVE YOURSELF PERMISSION

It's hugely important to give yourself permission (whether that's verbally or written) to: do the daily steps in this book, be/have/do/say/believe whatever you need to so that you can heal yourself, give yourself unlimited tries as many times as it takes, believe in your own worth and value, choose to create a life you love because you matter. Whenever you feel like you need someone else's permission to make a choice about your life, you just give that permission to yourself. The only permission you ever need to live your own life is your own.

YOU'RE ON A JOURNEY

It doesn't matter how old you are, how many times you've tried, or how far there is left to go. It's never too late to be the person you want to be. It's okay if you don't know things yet. You're on a journey and you'll figure it out as you go. This coloring book is designed to help you do just that.

BEGIN YOUR DAY WITH A STEP

If at all possible, do your daily step shortly after you wake up. That way, you'll be able to focus on yourself (because you're absolutely worth the time to do that) before your day gets away from you. So grab your favorite beverage. Find a quiet place. Relax and reflect while you're being creative.

IT'S A PRACTICE & A PROCESS

There's no doing this perfectly, and that's okay. You strive for progress. You do the best you can. So show yourself some patience and kindness because self-compassion is what you most need to heal yourself. You will make mistakes, there's just no way around it. Don't ever use any mistake as a reason to give up on yourself. Just circle back around and start again. And know this: every mistake is simply a brand new chance to do it better the next time.

AND FINALLY . . .

Remember (not just for this book but for all of life): you get out what you put in. So make yourself a priority in your own life because: 1. you're absolutely worth the effort and 2. no one else can do it for you. And one last suggestion good both for this book and for all of life: be brave and color outside the lines, that's where freedom lies.

THOSE WHO ARE BRAVE ARE FREE!

"It is not the critic who counts; not the man who points out how the strong man stumbles, or where the doer of deeds could have done them better. The credit belongs to the man who is actually in the arena, whose face is marred by dust and sweat and blood; who strives valiantly; who errs, who comes short again and again, because there is no effort without error and shortcoming; but who does actually strive to do the deeds; who knows great enthusiasms, the great devotions; who spends himself in a worthy cause; who at the best knows in the end the triumph of high achievement, and who at the worst, if he fails, at least fails while daring greatly, so that his place shall never be with those cold and timid souls who neither know victory nor defeat."

— Theodore Roosevelt

Source: excerpt (also known as *The Man In The Arena*) from the speech "Citizenship in a Republic" delivered at The Sorbonne in Paris, France on April 23, 1910.

COLOR TEST PAGE

COLOR TEST PAGE

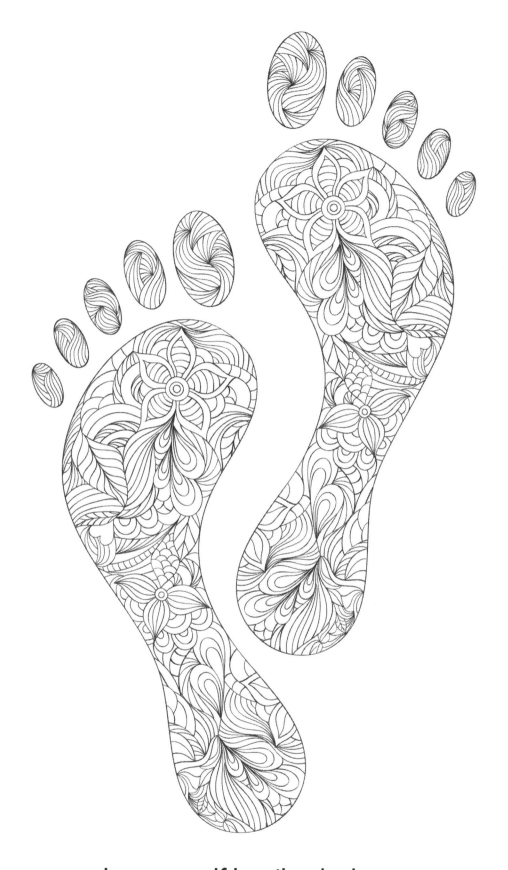

Let yourself be silently drawn
by the strange pull of what you really love.
It will not lead you astray.
—Jalaluddin Rumi

1

1. Today, relax.
2. Take a deep breath in through your nose.
3. Hold it for three seconds.
4. Let it out through your mouth.
5. Then pull your shoulders down away from your ears.
6. Repeat five times.
7. Massage your temples & the back of your neck.
8. Repeat often, especially every time you feel overwhelmed.

2

1. Today, know that you are not alone.
2. You may feel alone. You may feel like everyone else has it all together, is happy, & is moving forward while you are overwhelmed & exhausted.
3. But know this: you are likely comparing your insides to other people's outsides &/or comparing others' highlight reels to your everyday life.
4. So don't be so hard on yourself. Instead, remind yourself that you're not alone, that you are in fact in excellent company with the rest of us who are/ have been burned out, as often as needed.

3

1. Today, prioritize you.
2. Write your daily to-do list.
3. Now write your name at the very top of that list.
4. Know this: if you don't prioritize yourself and your needs (including doing activities that fulfill you) *every day* (regardless of how busy you may be), you will remain a burned-out husk of who you once were until you do.
5. Know this too: you are worth carving out time for yourself in your schedule. Your health & well-being matter because you matter. I assure you both of those things are true.

1. Today, slow down.
2. Take at least 15 minutes today to be alone & sit somewhere peaceful with your favorite beverage. Light some candles &/or turn on some music if you like. Relax. Rejuvenate. Refresh.
3. Take a deep breath in through your nose, hold it three seconds, let it out through your mouth. Pull your shoulders down away from your ears.
4. Let yourself just be right where you are, right here, right now.
5. Know this: if you don't come to a stop *at least once a day* to relax & enjoy your life, you'll remain a burned-out husk of who you once were until you do.

5

1. Today, listen to & heal your body.
2. Pay attention to how your body feels. Do you have tightness anywhere? Are you experiencing pain or achiness? Are you tired? Are you hungry/thirsty?
3. Write an answer to this: *What do I most need to do today to heal my body?*
4. The answers might be: hydrate, take a nap, go to the doctor, sit with the sun on your face, take a walk, stretch, make better food choices, etcetera.
5. It's your body. You know it better than anyone else. Trust yourself.
6. Know this: if you don't listen to your body & don't take care of yourself *every day*, you will remain a burned-out husk of who you once were until you do.

6

1. Today, take a break & play.
2. Write a list of activities that are fun & playful for you. Play consists of things you enjoy doing for the sake of doing them without any expectation of gain or a certain outcome.
3. This list can include anything that makes you happy, allows you to be free & let go for a little while, takes your mind off whatever else is going on in your life, & has no strings attached.
4. Pick one activity & do it today, guilt-free. Have fun & repeat often!

Prioritize you. Slow down. Do what your body most needs to heal itself.

7

1. Today, listen for your voice of wisdom (also known as your intuition).
2. Know this: your voice of wisdom is the one that's kind & nurturing & supportive. It'll *always* strengthen you & encourage you & help you grow.
3. So take at least 15 minutes out of your day to be alone. Be still & quiet. Ask this: *What words do I most need to hear right now?* Write your answer. Now ask any other questions that you want answers to. Listen for your intuition & write down the answers as they come (so no overthinking &/or editing).
4. Know this: all the answers you need truly are inside you. So trust yourself.

Prioritize you. Slow down. Do what your body most needs to heal itself.

8

1. Today, let yourself be silently drawn by the pull of what you really love.
2. Know this: you & you alone are responsible for your own happiness.
3. So get still & quiet then answer these: *What do I love to do, what lights a spark in me, what fulfills me? What am I doing when I'm at my happiest & when I feel the most alive?* Listen for that kind voice of wisdom inside you for the answers. Write the first things that come to you (so no overthinking &/or editing). Write down everything (big or small) that brings you joy.
4. Let your happiness & what you really love be your guides from now on.

Prioritize you. Slow down. Do what your body most needs to heal itself.

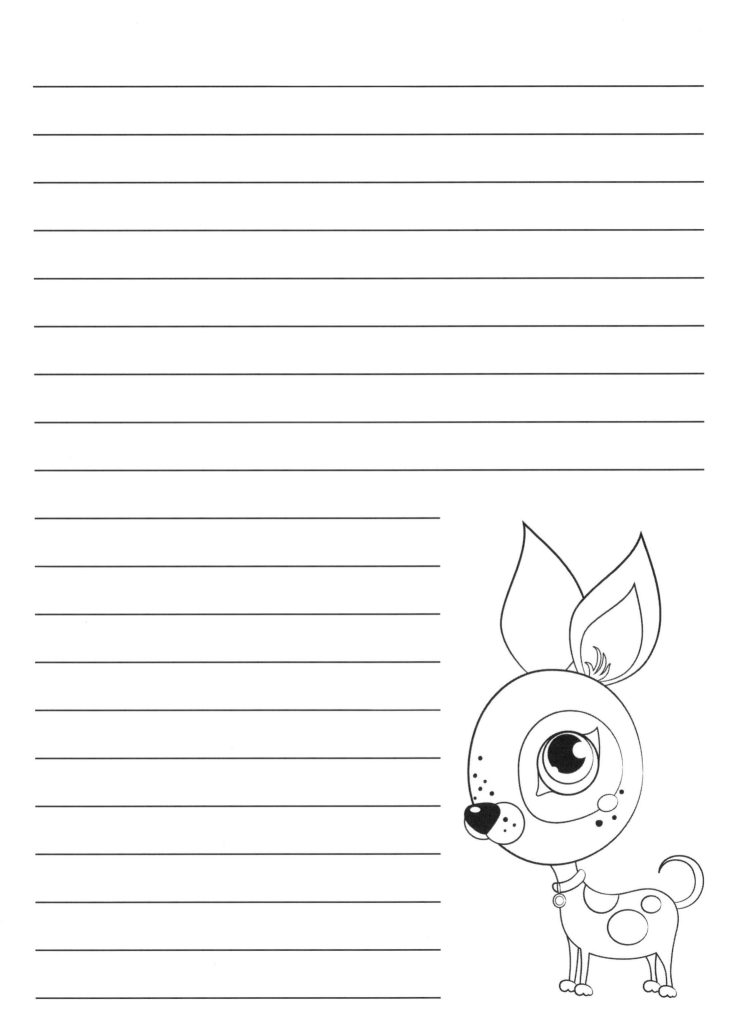

9

1. Today, believe that you're supported everywhere you go.
2. Write a list of instances in your life where you got help/money/guidance/ knowledge/relationships/etcetera when you most needed it (& put a star beside those you weren't expecting).
3. Now write this, say it aloud, & believe it: *Everything, in the end, works out for my good to help me grow into the person I'm meant to be.*
4. So choose to lower the stakes on how your life turns out. Take the pressure off. You don't have to do it all. Life guides & supports you.

Prioritize you. Slow down. Do what your body most needs to heal itself.

10

1. Today, make some choices.
2. Write your daily to-do list. Put your name at the top.
3. Know this: you're exchanging your life for the things you choose to do with your time. Answer this: *Do I want more exhaustion or more fulfillment?*
4. Put a star next to those things on your to-do list that are most important to you & that you, yourself, must do. Circle those things you can delegate to others. Finally, cross out those things that aren't important to you at all.
5. Take action & delegate today. Let go, guilt-free, of the crossed-out items.

Prioritize you. Slow down. Do what your body most needs to heal itself.

11

1. Today, come alive.
2. Look at your edited daily schedule from Day 10.
3. Now read through your answers from Day 8.
4. You've freed up some of your time, so now where can you add in some of the things that: you really love/create a spark in you/fulfill you/make you happy/you want to be doing with your life so that you'll feel the most alive?
5. Add at least one of those things onto your schedule today & go do it.
6. Do something (no matter how big or small) that fulfills you *every day*.

Prioritize you. Slow down. Do what your body most needs to heal itself.

12

1. Today, nourish your body.
2. Write a quick list of your favorite foods (ones you are able to eat).
3. Now listen to your body.
4. When you're hungry, choose one of your favorite foods & prepare it *exactly* the way you like.
5. Sit somewhere quiet & relaxed then eat slowly. Savor the taste!
6. Stop when you're comfortably full. Save or discard any leftovers.
7. Do all this guilt-free!

Prioritize you. Slow down. Heal your body. Do something that fulfills you.

13

1. Today, exercise your body.
2. Know this: the right exercise for you is the one that you'll do.
3. Write a quick list of a few exercises you enjoy. (Keep in mind: *anything* that gets you moving & your heart rate elevated is exercise.)
4. Pick your favorite exercise & do it for at least 15 minutes if you're able. Do it alone or grab a friend to keep you company.
5. Repeat often, especially when you feel burned out. (Fact: exercise increases biochemicals in your brain that make you happier & less stressed).

Prioritize you. Slow down. Heal your body. Do something that fulfills you.

14

1. Today, make boundaries.
2. Write this down: *No is a complete sentence. No.*
3. Know this: you don't have to negotiate your refusal with anyone or explain yourself or give excuses why you can't. All you have to say is: *No.*
4. Keeping in mind that you are the top priority on your to-do list now, politely say *no* to anything that you don't want/need/have time to do.
5. Know this too: you create the life you're living. So make & enforce your own boundaries until you create a life that is manageable & enjoyable for you.

Prioritize you. Slow down. Heal your body. Do something that fulfills you.

15

1. Today, answer who.
2. Write the answer to these: *Who am I living & doing & making choices for on a regular basis; is it for me? Who is my motivation? Who am I allowing in my head (parent/spouse/boss/etcetera), telling me that I'm selfish for having needs of my own? Who am I afraid to upset by making myself & my happiness a priority?*
3. This is not just about your daily to-do list but also about your long-term vision for who you would like to become.

Prioritize you. Slow down. Heal your body. Do something that fulfills you.

16

1. Today, answer why.
2. Write the answer to these: *Why am I putting others before myself? Why isn't my own happiness, fulfillment, & well-being paramount? Why do I believe that my wants & needs matter less?*
3. Know this: you can't take excellent care of others unless you take excellent care of yourself first. Making your own well-being your sole motivation will make it easier for you to let yourself be drawn by what you really love so you can come alive. That, in turn, will make you genuinely excited about your life.

Prioritize you. Slow down. Heal your body. Do something that fulfills you.

17

1. Today, answer what.
2. Write the answer to these: *What matters deeply to me? What do I really, truly love? What do I most want to be doing with my life? What activities make me feel the most alive? What is my heart telling me? What is my voice of wisdom telling me right now? What do I want to experience during my lifetime? What do I want to my legacy to be when I am gone?*

Prioritize you. Slow down. Heal your body. Do something that fulfills you.

18

1. Today, answer when.
2. Write the answer to these: *When will I look at my life as my own? When will I listen to my own heart? When will I take responsibility for my own happiness? When will I give myself permission to be/do/have/say what I want? When will I choose to take action & step out in faith instead of backing down in fear? When will I realize that the "right time" is right now?*
3. Then answer this (especially for anything that matters to you that you're telling yourself you'll get to later): *If not now, then when?*

Prioritize you. Slow down. Heal your body. Do something that fulfills you.

19

1. Today, answer where.
2. Write the answer to these: *Where am I when I'm at my happiest? Where do I need to be to pursue those things that deeply matter to me? Where do I feel the most at home? Where do I feel the most alive? Where do I most want to go from here?*

Prioritize you. Slow down. Heal your body. Do something that fulfills you.

20

1. Today, answer how.
2. Write the answer to this: *How do I get from where I am now to where I most want to be?*
3. Hint: start with where you most want to be & work your way backward to today. I know you're exhausted so think small, very small. Don't scare or overwhelm yourself. Just answer this: *What small (tiny if need be & therefore completely doable) actions/steps do I need to take so I can let myself be drawn by what I really love, do what I really love, come alive, & have a life that excites me?*

Prioritize you. Slow down. Heal your body. Do something that fulfills you.

21

1. Today, befriend yourself.
2. Know this: you are with you 24/7. You are the closest & best friend you'll ever have. Letting yourself get/remain burned out is not being a friend to yourself; rather, it's an act of self-abuse.
3. So resolve today to have your own back *always*. Choose to take excellent care of yourself every day, just like a good friend would.
4. Now go do something nice for yourself. Take the day off or go shopping just for you or read a book or whatever will make you feel nourished & cared for.

Prioritize you. Slow down. Heal your body. Do something that fulfills you.

22

1. Today, come alive again.
2. Read through your list from Day 8.
3. Pick an activity that brings you joy & do it today.
4. Let loose for a little while. Take your mind off everything.
5. Have fun!

Prioritize you. Slow down. Heal your body. Do something that fulfills you.

23

1. Today, take action.
2. Read through your answers from Days 15-20.
3. Now you know who you're living for, why you're doing what you're doing, what you really love, & where you want to be headed. You've written an action plan on how to get to a life that excites you & makes you feel alive.
4. Take a deep breath in through your nose, hold briefly, let it out your mouth.
5. Now it's time: take the first (tiny if need be) step in that plan & move forward.
6. Repeat *every day*: one deep breath & the next small step in your Day 20 plan.

Prioritize you. Slow down. Heal your body. Do something that fulfills you.

24

1. Today, be grateful.
2. Write a list of at least five things that you love about your life &/or that are good in your life.
3. Reread. See the abundance in your life now.
4. Choose to believe even more good things are coming your way (because they are). Believe that *every day* (even if you can't see it right now) & it will come to pass.
5. Now take a deep breath & do the next small (tiny) step in your Day 20 plan.

Prioritize you. Slow down. Heal your body. Do something that fulfills you.

25

1. Today, refresh.
2. Go hang out with a person/pet you love or at least like a whole lot.
3. Do something that you'll both enjoy.
4. Stay in the moment & belly laugh at least once.
5. Have a great time!
6. Repeat often.
7. Then take a deep breath & do the next small (tiny) step in your Day 20 plan.

Prioritize you. Slow down. Heal your body. Do something that fulfills you.

26

1. Today, recognize the vampires.
2. Know this: a vampire is a person/place/thing that sucks the life/energy right out of you.
3. Write a list of vampires in your life. You'll know them by the negative way your body reacts &/or feels when you're around them. Now, beside each one, write why you're allowing these exhausting people/places/things in your life. (Hint: what do you hope to gain by staying in their presence?)
4. Then take a deep breath & do the next small (tiny) step in your Day 20 plan.

Prioritize you. Slow down. Heal your body. Do something that fulfills you.

27

1. Today, let go.
2. Read through your list from Day 26.
3. Choose (yes, it's a choice) to do yourself a kindness today & *every day* by limiting your time with vampire people/places/things or cut them out of your life entirely. Letting them go is a practice & a process. Start today.
4. Should you feel guilty about doing that, always remember: it's your mental health (& your own life) that you're working to save.
5. Then take a deep breath & do the next small (tiny) step in your Day 20 plan.

Prioritize you. Slow down. Heal your body. Do something that fulfills you.

1. Today, change what you think.
2. Choose to look at your feelings of burnout as a kind of guidance system. They're simply telling you that: 1. you're headed in the wrong direction & 2. you're not meeting your own needs.
3. Do another (tiny if need be) step in your Day 20 plan. Remember: that's the direction in which you most want to be headed because what you most need is to be drawn by what you really love, to do what you really love, & to come alive. So keep moving forward with your plan a little more every day.

Prioritize you. Slow down. Heal your body. Do something that fulfills you.

28

29

1. Today, say yes.
2. Write this: *I say yes to taking excellent care of myself. I say yes to letting myself relax. I say yes to being drawn by & to doing what I really love. I say yes to all those things that bring me joy & fulfill me. I say yes to coming alive & having a life I love.*
3. Then add anything else you'd like to say yes to.
4. Remember: choose to believe that life is trying to help you, that everything, in the end, works in your favor. And *always* believe something good is coming your way because it is; you just have to say *yes* to it first.

Prioritize you. Slow down. Heal your body. Do something that fulfills you.

Congratulations!

30

1. Today, celebrate!
2. Be proud of yourself for how far you've come.
3. Write down your successes & victories (big or small).
4. Do something nice for yourself (like a prize for a job well done).
5. Go & enjoy your life!

Prioritize you. Slow down. Heal your body. Do something that fulfills you.

ABOUT THE AUTHOR!

This book was born out of Shelli Johnson's own struggle with burnout. She wanted and needed to heal herself. She wanted and needed practical and easy steps she could take to find what made her come alive and then go do it so she could find happiness in her life again. So she simply wrote the book she needed to read. Every day, she does her best to cut herself some slack & practice progress, not perfection.

Shelli's also an award-winning journalist (sports reporting), novelist (grand prize winner), and blogger (shellijohnson.com/blog). She's a truck owner, horse rider, photographer, yoga enthusiast, and slow-cooker fan (shellijohnson.com/recipes). Find out more at: shellijohnson.com/about

Find out about Shelli's other books at:
shellijohnson.com/books

GET YOUR FREE STUFF!

Visit: shellijohnson.com/signup
Opt-in for the newsletter to keep in touch.
Get a free bookmark to color.

ACKNOWLEDGMENTS!

My sincere thanks to people who make my days brighter:
Rollin Johnson
Heather Porazzo

The book's content is not a substitute for direct, personal, professional medical care and diagnosis. None of the exercises or treatments (including products and services) mentioned in this book should be performed or otherwise used without prior approval from your physician or other qualified professional health care provider.

There may be risks associated with participating in activities or using products and services mentioned in this book for people in poor health or with pre-existing physical or mental health conditions.

Because these risks exist, you will not use such products or participate in such activities if you are in poor health or have a pre-existing mental or physical condition. If you choose to participate in these risks, you do so of your own free will and accord, knowingly and voluntarily assuming all risks associated with such activities.

Earnings & Income Disclaimers
No Earnings Projections, Promises or Representations
For purposes of these disclaimers, the term "Author" refers individually and collectively to the author of this book and to the affiliate (if any) whose affiliate hyperlinks are referenced in this book.

You recognize and agree that the Author and the Publisher have made no implications, warranties, promises, suggestions, projections, representations or guarantees whatsoever to you about future prospects or earnings, or that you will earn any money, with respect to your purchase of this book, and that the Author and the Publisher have not authorized any such projection, promise, or representation by others.

Any earnings or income statements, or any earnings or income examples, are only estimates of what you might earn. There is no assurance you will do as well as stated in any examples. If you rely upon any figures provided, you must accept the entire risk of not doing as well as the information provided. This applies whether the earnings or income examples are monetary in nature or pertain to advertising credits which may be earned (whether such credits are convertible to cash or not).

There is no assurance that any prior successes or past results as to earnings or income (whether monetary or advertising credits, whether convertible to cash or not) will apply, nor can any prior successes be used, as an indication of your future success or results from any of the information, content, or strategies. Any and all claims or representations as to income or earnings (whether monetary or advertising credits, whether convertible to cash or not) are not to be considered as "average earnings".

Testimonials & Examples
Testimonials and examples in this book are exceptional results, do not reflect the typical purchaser's experience, do not apply to the average person and are not intended to represent or guarantee that anyone will achieve the same or similar results. Where specific income or earnings (whether monetary or advertising credits, whether convertible to cash or not), figures are used and attributed to a specific individual or business, that individual or business has earned that amount. There is no assurance that you will do as well using the same information or strategies. If you rely on the specific income or earnings figures used, you must accept all the risk of not doing as well. The described experiences are atypical. Your financial results are likely to differ from those described in the testimonials.

The Economy
The economy, where you do business, on a national and even worldwide scale, creates additional uncertainty and economic risk. An economic recession or depression might negatively affect your results.

Your Success or Lack of It
Your success in using the information or strategies provided in this book depends on a variety of factors. The Author and the Publisher have no way of knowing how well you will do because they do not know you, your background, your work ethic, your dedication, your motivation, your desire, or your business skills or practices. Therefore, neither the Author nor the Publisher guarantees or implies that you will get rich, that you will do as well, or that you will have any earnings (whether monetary or advertising credits, whether convertible to cash or not), at all.

Businesses and earnings derived therefrom involve unknown risks and are not suitable for everyone. You may not rely on any information presented in this book or otherwise provided by the Author or the Publisher, unless you do so with the knowledge and understanding that you can experience significant losses (including, but not limited to, the loss of any monies paid to purchase this book and/or any monies spent setting up, operating, and/or marketing your business activities, and further, that you may have no earnings at all (whether monetary or advertising credits, whether convertible to cash or not).

Forward-Looking Statements
Materials in this book may contain information that includes or is based upon forward-looking statements within the meaning of the Securities Litigation Reform Act of 1995. Forward-looking statements give the Author's expectations or forecasts of future events. You can identify these statements by the fact that they do not relate strictly to historical or current facts. They use words such as "anticipate," "estimate," "expect," "project," "intend," "plan," "believe," and other words and terms of similar meaning in connection with a description of potential earnings or financial performance.

Any and all forward looking statements here or on any materials in this book are intended to express an opinion of earnings potential. Many factors will be important in determining your actual results and no guarantees are made that you will achieve results similar to the Author or anybody else. In fact, no guarantees are made that you will achieve any results from applying the Author's ideas, strategies, and tactics found in this book.

Purchase Price
Although the Publisher believes the price is fair for the value that you receive, you understand and agree that the purchase price for this book has been arbitrarily set by the Publisher or the vendor who sold you this book. This price bears no relationship to objective standards.

Due Diligence
You are advised to do your own due diligence when it comes to making any decisions. Use caution and seek the advice of qualified professionals before acting upon the contents of this book or any other information. You shall not consider any examples, documents, or other content in this book or otherwise provided by the Author or Publisher to be the equivalent of professional advice.

The Author and the Publisher assume no responsibility for any losses or damages resulting from your use of any link, information, or opportunity contained in this book or within any other information disclosed by the Author or the Publisher in any form whatsoever.

YOU SHOULD ALWAYS CONDUCT YOUR OWN INVESTIGATION (PERFORM DUE DILIGENCE)
BEFORE BUYING PRODUCTS OR SERVICES FROM ANYONE. THIS INCLUDES PRODUCTS AND SERVICES
SOLD VIA WEBSITE LINKS REFERENCED IN THIS BOOK.

93564007R00072

Made in the USA
Lexington, KY
16 July 2018